Rob Versus The Unicorns

Repelling The Mystical, Malevolent And Borderline Idiotic With Spells Of Sarcasm, Wit & Humor.

Rob Anspach

Rob Versus The Unicorns

Repelling The Mystical, Malevolent And Borderline Idiotic With Spells Of Sarcasm, Wit And Humor.

Copyright © 2022 Anspach Media
Cover design by: Freddy Solis

All rights reserved. No part of this book may be reproduced or transmitted in any form or by any means without written permission from the author.

ISBN 13: 978-1-7377355-4-0

Printed in USA

Disclaimer:
Oh yes, we must have a disclaimer…it makes the lawyers happy. The author has spent a lifetime using sarcasm as a means to grow his business. He shares interactions in this book that you may or may not agree with, his actions and communications are contrary to what most customer service gurus teach. But, it works for him and could work for you too, although highly doubtful.

What People Are Saying

"It seems like you've somehow hit a mythical level, where you manage to attract some of the dumbest people in the world."
~ **Manny Wolfe**

"There is a famous cartoon in which two unicorns miss their ride on Noah's Ark, exclaiming "Wait...that was today?" I believe Telemarketers and Scammers are the descendants of those unicorns, and they are still upset. And Rob Anspach may actually be the exponential-great-great-grand-nephew of Noah. That's why his phone keeps ringing. This book is out there NOW, my unicorn friends. Get your copy before it starts raining. Come aboard, grab a Vanilla Iced-Coffee and a grilled-cheese, and settle in for a laugh filled journey that could last 40 days and 40 nights...if you read slowly enough."
~ **Steve Gamlin,** The Motivational Firewood® Guy Speaker, Author, VisionBoarder

"I had to stop reading after 5 chapters because I couldn't see the pages from the tears of laughter pouring out of my eyes."
~ **Allan Gaskamp,** Trophies & More, www.trophiesmore.com

"I've enjoyed every book Rob Anspach has ever written. 'Rob Versus The Unicorns' is another in a long line of informative, funny and sarcastic ones. But read it carefully because, although it would be a good script for a stand-up comedian, it is filled with truisms that are applicable to many aspects of life!"
- **Ben Gay III,** Author of "The Closers"

"I have to be careful when I read anything Rob writes. I make sure I'm not drinking or eating because I know I won't be able to contain the laughter. Oh sure, initially I'm lulled into thinking these chuckles and a few giggles will be all I experience. Then there's that one line - out of nowhere - completely unexpected - that forces me into a belly laugh. The snark and sarcasm is alive and well in this book and I, for one, am looking forward to the next book that strikes blood pumping anxiety into the heart of every telemarketer, phone scammer, and newbie to social selling who blindly follows bad coaching advice.
– **Charlene Burke,** www.EmailWritingService.com

"Been reading Rob Anspach's latest book, Rob Vs the Unicorns. If you are in any sort of business, online or off, if you deal with customers, if you have a phone, if you are still breathing... run to your nearest book store and grab a copy. Whenever you feel like the turkeys are winning, this book and Rob will bring a smile to your lips, a lightness to your step and proof that justice is indeed served. Rob's stories are full of humor and insights, a powerful combination. And hopefully, you'll start firing clients who are PITA's a lot sooner, too!"
– **Scott Paton**, Podcast Director & Course Creator

"Funny shit!"
– **Randy Chaffee** exclaiming after reading the first four chapters.

"Rob's books have been a welcome breath of sarcastic air. Rob vs The Unicorns has people desperate to make it into his books and Rob doesn't disappoint in his replies to them."
–**Jonathan Thompson**, Director & Creative Consultant

"Bigger! Bolder! Funnier! Rob has angered every call center from Dubai to Portland. Once again, I'm laughing my you know what off!"
- **Brad Szollose**, Host of Awakened Nation

"I have the same problem with Rob Versus the Unicorns as I have with all of the Rob Versus books: I come away with a serious case of FOMO since I always decline spam calls and delete spam emails. With the perfect mix of sarcasm and wit, wily Rob teaches valuable lessons in protecting yourself and communicating more effectively - and you even get to see words like "whippersnapper" in print. The last time I heard that word was when my mother had Alzheimer's, so I got the extra joy of a heartwarming memory from this book. No telling what treasures you may pull from it! But don't complain to Rob if you find none, unless you want to be in his next Rob Versus book."
 - **Lisa Kipps-Brown**, Author of "Disrupt Your Now"

"I've always loved reading the books in the Rob Versus series and Rob Versus The Unicorns does not disappoint. It's impossible not to have a great laugh as Rob shares real life example of interactions he's had with unsuspecting scammers where he gets to fully use his gift of sarcasm. This is another entertaining read that also provides we entrepreneurs with plenty of examples on how NOT to treat our prospects and clients. Thanks for yet another great read Rob!"
 - **Kevin Thompson**, Tribe For Leaders www.TribeForLeaders.com

Table of Contents

Introduction 9
Chapter 1 - The Man, The Myth. Yeah, Something Like That! 11
Hey Rob, Your Books Suck! 12
The Bro Code 14
Keep Trying 15
Is This Robert? 17
Say My Name 18
Just Read The Script 21
Chapter 2 - Fraudulent Activity You Say? 25
He Really Didn't Want To Talk About It 26
I Have A Suggestion 29
Chapter 3 - It's My Goal In Life 33
It's The FRCA Calling 34
Funding Denied 36
Sir, You're Poop! 38
Chapter 4 - It's What I Do 43
The Quote Was High 44
My Boss Wants A Quote 46
Chapter 5 - Being Sociable...Sort Of! 49
It's None Of Your Darn Business 50
YouTube Is Not For Whippersnappers 52
Show Me The Money 54
He Found Me, Then Blocked Me 55
You Need Something Alright 57
Retired And Blocked 60
Bugger Off 62
Oh Yeah…Could Be! 63

 Pfft…He Wasn't Civil! 65

 Invited Then Blocked 66

 Hello LinkedIn Loser…Goodbye! 68

Chapter 6 - Life Choices 71

 Split Personality 72

 Medicare You Say 75

 Just Wanting To Argue 78

 Never Gonna Happen! 81

Chapter 7 - He Who Shall Be Named 85

 Voldemort For The Win 86

 The Guy With Many Questions 88

Chapter 8 - This Is The Sci-Fi Chapter 91

 All Too Easy 92

 Long Live Flash 94

 It's The Sarcasm's Fault 96

Chapter 9 - Saturday Shenanigans 99

 Grilled Sarcasm 100

 Yeah, I'm The Imposter 103

Chapter 10 - Attitude Adjustments Needed 107

 Arrogant & Cocky 108

 The Postal Rules 110

 Training Day 112

 It's a Matter Of Urgency 114

Chapter 11 - If Only They Were Honest 117

 Nope 118

 Not Yet 120

 To Be Or Not To Be…Forthright! 126

 Slower And Louder 128

I Need Your Name... 129
Henceforth Your Name Is Cheeto 131
Chapter 12 - Hey, They're My Superpowers. 133
It Depends.. 134
Indian Voice 137
No Hortons For Me 138
Third Time... 140
Apparently You Are Calling Me Obnoxious................................... 142
About The Author.. 145
Resources 146

Introduction

"Hi Rob, thanks for the connection."

Typical start of a spammy pitch into my social media inbox, which is followed by, "I have a program (course, book, offer, or whatever)" that they then want to jump on a call, have me click a link or watch some video.

And it usually ends with me being cursed at and blocked because I hurt their feelings with my sarcasm.

If only they had read my "Rob Versus" books first, they would know exactly how to enter into a conversation with me, sell more of whatever they're shilling that day, and actually try to win at the "build a relationship first" game.

Fortunately for me, most of those who engage in such foolishness will never learn and their stories just end up in more of my books. Huzzah!

And you the reader get to experience that interaction as if you were there in that very moment. So get ready to smile, laugh and howl as you spend an hour or so reading through my further adventures.

Enjoy.

Rob

Rob Anspach
Anspach Media
www.AnspachMedia.com

"You know what never saved the planet? Your sarcasm!"
~ Phastos to Sprite –
from the Marvel movie "The Eternals"

"Pfft…my sarcasm has definitely saved the planet."
~ Rob Anspach

Chapter 1

The Man, The Myth…
Yeah, Something Like That!

"I've become that guy…accept it!"

Hey Rob, Your Books Suck!

{Message appears in my Facebook inbox}

Me: Ah, so you read them?

Them: Yeah.

Me: How many of my books did you read?

Them: All of your Rob Versus books plus some others.

Me: And every one of them sucked?

Them: Yeah.

Me: So if you felt the first one you read sucked, why did you read more?

Them: At first I wasn't sure what I felt, but the more I read the more I knew they sucked.

Me: Sounds like you have a problem then.

Them: What's that?

Me: You should stop reading books that suck.

Them: How will I know if they suck if I don't read them?

Me: I suppose that's a risk you will have to take.

Them: Yeah.

Me: I have more Rob Versus books coming out, should I put your name on the list for an advanced copy?

Them: Yeah, that would be nice.

Me: Even if they suck?

Them: I won't know if they suck until I read them.

Me: Ah, so my books don't suck in the sense you don't like them, but rather suck as in "suck you in" or draw you in to keep reading?

Them: That's what I've been saying, for a guy who writes books, you're really dumb.

Me: You're right, I should completely understand what people are thinking when they say, "your books suck".

Them: Exactly. They do.

Me: Ugh.

Note: I'm sure I could've chatted with this weirdo for hours, but I wasn't emotionally or mentally prepared to take that journey. So I felt it best just to stop responding.

The Bro Code

The other morning I drove to the local gas station to fill up the car.

Before I left though, I contemplated wearing a hat as my hair was all over the place.

Pfft, "who cares", I thought, "it's just hair...and seriously ain't nobody gonna care".

So I pull up at the pump and notice two other fellas pumping gas.

Both were wearing hats.

Both looked at me like I was the guy who did something wrong.

Like I broke the bro code or.

The first guy gets in his car and I could see him adjusting his rear view mirror to watch me, then he drove away.

The second guy just stares at me for a moment, then in a loud obnoxious voice says, "wear a hat next time."

And he gets in his car and speeds away.

Note: Pfft...The one day I don't wear a hat and I get hat shamed.

Keep Trying

Phone rings... caller I.D. displays a Metairie LA number.

{Oh, I already know it's a scammer, but I answer it anyway}

Me: This is Rob, how can I help you with your scam today.

{The caller apparently didn't hear me and continued with his intro}

Caller: This is Mike from Senior Advocate Services.

Me: Mike from where?

Caller: I'm Mike from Senior Advocate Services.

Me: Okay and…

Caller: If you agree I can have a representative call you in a few days to review our many life insurance options.

Me: Well Mike, can you tell me where you're calling me from?

Caller: Pennsylvania, of course.

Me: That's amazing. But how's the weather in Louisiana this morning?

Caller: It's 84 degrees, but we're supposed to get more rain soon.

Me: That's nice. So you're not in Pennsylvania then?

Caller: {slight pause} You f**cker!

Me: Keep trying…one day even you Mike might be able to scam me…but not today.

{Mike started to say something, but I heard in the background another person tell Mike "it's not worth it" and to just hang up.}

Note: Mike, if you're reading this…it's worth it…it totally is. I mean seriously, without you and all your scammer buddies this whole series of books wouldn't exist. So yeah…worth it.

Is This Robert?

Phone rings… Caller ID is blank which is odd.
{I know it's a scam, but I can't resist answering it}

Me: Hello.

Caller: Is this Robert?
{He says in a thick foreign accent}

Me: Yep.

Caller: A Mr. Robert Anspach?

Me: That's right.

Caller: F**k!

{And he hung up}

Note: I really hate when scammers don't allow me to waste their time with my sarcasm. I just don't feel appreciated.

Say My Name

Phone rings…Caller ID displays "PNC Bank - Gettysburg PA"

{I know it's a scam…but I answer it anyway}

Me: Hello.
{Automated message plays… "Please hold to discuss your Google My Business listing"}

Phone Rep: Hi, whom may I ask is it that I'm speaking to?

Me: It's me the person you called.

Phone Rep: Can you be more specific?

Me: More specific than what?

Phone Rep: Do you have a name?

Me: Of course.

Phone Rep: Can I have it?

Me: No, it's my name.

Phone Rep: What is your name so I can verify who you are?

Me: I know who I am, so consider it verified.

Phone Rep: Are you the owner of {gives the name of some business I never heard of}?

Me: Yup.

Phone Rep: Well we need to update your Google My Business listing.

Me: Who's we?

Phone Rep: Oh, we is the company I work for.

Me: Of which you haven't stated your name or the name of the company you represent.

Phone Rep: Thought I did at the beginning.

Me: Beginning of time, or the beginning of this call?

Phone Rep: When you picked up the phone I introduced myself.

Me: Nope, never happened.

Phone Rep: It certainly did happen.

Me: Well, tell me again.

Phone Rep: I already did.

Me: No, you didn't.

Phone Rep: I think you just want to argue with me.

Me: I would never dream of arguing with you.

Phone Rep: You are doing it right now.

Me: It's not arguing…it's called wasting your time…there's a difference.

Phone Rep: You're an a-hole.

Me: Pfft…you don't even know me.

Phone Rep: I know who you are.

Me: Really? Say my name?

Phone Rep: Um…Er…

Me: {impersonating Walter "Heisenberg" White from the TV show Breaking Bad} SAY MY NAME! SAY IT!

{He hung up}

Note: In most cases they have no idea who you are and are relying on you to give them the information they need to rip you off. Don't reveal anything…just waste their time.

Just Read The Script

House phone rings…Caller ID shows a local number.

Me: Hello.

Them: Is this Robert?

Me: Speaking.

Them: {Slight pause} Is this Robert?

Me: You already asked and I answered.

Them: {Again another pause} Robert?

Me: I said it was. Can you move on to the next question?

Them: Hmm, err, huh?

Me: You called me, so evidently you have something to tell me, sell me or scam me…so proceed with reading your script.

Them: {Again another pause then} Err, umm.

Me: Read the script.

Them: Oh right, sorry Sir. Nervous.

Me: Why?

Them: My boss and colleagues warned me about you, I just didn't think I'd get you on the phone my first week.

Me: Am I as horrible as they make me out to be?

Them: No, not yet.

Me: Okay now, read the script.

Them: Sir, Mr. Robert Sir.

Me: {I really wanted at this point to go all Sam Kinison on him and scream
"Read The Script, Read It"
but I just said instead...}
Well you either are offering a lower credit card rate, lower electric bills, a warranty of some sort or solar panels...which one?

Them: Yes.

Me: Which one?

Them: Yes.

Me: Read the script.

Them: I can't, I'm nervous.

Me: {and Sam Kinison found his way out}
"READ THE SCRIPT, READ IT!"

Them: {Longer pause this time}

Me: Did I scare you?

{Wait for it...}

Them: FFFF...FFFF*** You!

{And then he hung up}

Note: Honestly these are calls I enjoy the most. Why? Because in most cases I either frustrate them, scare them or make them want to quit scamming people. It's their "Come to Rob" moment. And I have to believe I'm making a difference in curbing the scam callers somehow.

Chapter 2

Fraudulent Activity You Say?

"Oh yeah, seems totally legit!"

He Really Didn't Want To Talk About It

Phone rings… Caller ID displays local bank.

{But it was a holiday and I know they are closed…so yeah a scam…but I answer it anyway.}

Me: Hello.

Caller: This is Jim from Card Services, I'm calling to let you know that your credit card might have been fraudulently used, so we need to check to make sure those charges were legitimate.

Me: Oh no, sounds awful.

Caller: Can you verify the last 4 digits of your card.

Me: Which card?

Caller: Your Mastercard.

Me: Okay, but there is no numbers on it, just my name.

Caller: Say again.

Me: I have the Apple branded Mastercard by Goldman Sachs and it has no numbers on the card, just a digital chip on the front and a magnetic stripe on the back.

Caller: Well F-you then.

Me: So I take it my card wasn't compromised?

Caller: I hate people like you.

Me: Do you want to talk about it? I'm here for you.

Caller: Um, er, hmmm….

Me: Use your words.

Caller: {Curses at me in some foreign language}

Me: Yes, let it out, you will feel so much better. {Slight pause - then a second voice comes on the phone}

Caller 2: We will get your information sooner or later.

Me: Put Jim back on the phone, I think we were having a break through moment.

Caller 2: You a-hole, all you do is waste our time. Stop answering the phone.

Me: Then stop calling me.

Caller: 2: My people need training.

Me: Exactly and what better way than by having me answer the calls and getting them used to rejection and their time wasted.

Caller 2: Stop answering the calls.

Me: Stop calling me then.

{Pfft, he hung up}

Note: Unless you positively know beyond a shadow of a doubt that it is indeed your bank calling, never ever give out your credit card information over the phone to a total stranger. Why? Because it's a scam.

I Have A Suggestion

House phone rings...

{Very few call me on the house phone, so it's usually a scam call.}

...I answer it anyway.

Me: Hello.

Automated message plays "We have detected fraudulent activity on your CashApp account press 1 to speak to a CashApp representative."

{So I press 1}

{Some beeping noises, then I get a real person...with a foreign accent}

Me: Hello.

Rep: This is CashApp, can I ask why you are calling?

Me: Your system called me.

Rep: We detected fraudulent activity on your account coming from Boston, Dallas and Detroit, have you been to these places?

Me: I have been there yes, just not in the last few weeks.

Rep: Are you using the app now?

Me: No, I'm on the phone with you.

Rep: Do you use an iPhone or Android device?

Me: Yes.

Rep: Which one do you use...iPhone or Android?

Me: Both.

Rep: Which one are you using right now on this call?

Me: Neither.

Rep: How can you be talking to me if you are not using either your iPhone or Android phone?

Me: Magic.

Rep: Sir, I don't think you are taking this serious.

{Me making a serious face}

Me: Okay, I'm serious now.

Rep: Sir, can we get back to your account?

Me: Why?

Rep: We are trying to help you?

Me: No, I don't think you are.

Rep: Sir, can I make a suggestion?

Me: No, but I have a suggestion... you can stick that scam of yours up your...

{Pfft, he hung up}

Note: Always be suspicious of callers who want you to verify your information but never ask if you are the person intended for the call. They never ask for you personally or any member of the household, they automatically assume you are the person in question. Nah, scam.

Chapter 3

It's My Goal In Life

"Or an obsession…the verdict is still out on that!"

It's The FRCA Calling

Phone rings...caller ID says "Unknown"
{But I answered it anyway}

Me: Ay-oh.

Them: Hi, this is James from the FRCA.

Me: Does that stand for "Fellowship of the Royal College of Anesthetists?

Them: What?

Me: How about the "Florida Regional Councils Association?"

Them: Sir, can you stop talking so I can explain?

Me: Okay my first two guesses were wrong, let me try one more time... how about "First Regional Compost Authority".

Them: Sir, none of them were correct.

Me: Well then what do you want?

Them: I want to help you reduce your debt.

Me: How do you know I have any debt?

Them: We are the FRCA we know everything.

Me: Are you a member of the Freaking Ridiculous Callers Anonymous group?

Them: Kiss my ass you're not interested in my service, you just want to waste my time.

Me: What gave it away?

{Pfft, he hung up}

Note: Oh yes, my goal in life is wasting scam caller's time. I mean really, it is…and the conversations make great stories, so there's that.

Funding Denied

My mobile rings…Caller ID displays Greensboro FL {most likely a scam…but I answer anyway}

Me: Hello.
{no one answers…although I can hear tapping sounds}

Me: Hello.
{more tapping}

Caller: Hello.

Me: That's what I said.

Caller: Oh, is this Lee?

Me: {I didn't want to disappoint} Yup, who's this?

Caller: My name's Kevin from Capital Funding.

Me: Okay and?

Kevin: Does your business need funding?

Me: What kind of funding?

Kevin: We lend businesses funds over $10,000.

Me: Okay, so how much are you going to lend me?

Kevin: How much do you need?

Me: What's the limit?

Kevin: We can lend up to 20 million.

Me: Okay I'll take that.

Kevin: And what would you do with 20 million?

Me: Do I need to tell you?

Kevin: Yes, we need to know what you plan on doing with the money before we loan it to you.

Me: Well I'm going to have a big ole' crack party and invite all my friends.

Kevin: Hmm, err, huh.

Me: You're welcome to come to the party I'm sure there will be plenty.

Kevin: Of crack?

Me: Yeah, that's right.
{wait for it....}

Kevin: F-You!

Me: So no loan then?

{and he hung up}

Sir, You're Poop!

Mobile phone rings…Caller ID displays "Altus Global Recv"

Me: Hello.

{click, the caller hangs up}

{a minute goes by}

Mobile phone rings…same Caller ID information

Me: Hello.

Caller: Sorry Sir, my phone disconnected on my last call. I'm Robert with Debt Recovery Solutions. Do you require assistance in collecting past due invoices?

Me: Hmm, nope.

Caller: Wow, I've spoken to many companies and they all seem to require assistance in some fashion. What's your secret?

Me: I just a call a number…and within 3 days the outstanding invoices are paid.

Caller: Three days?

Me: Yup, sometimes sooner.

Caller: And what's the fee they charge?

Me: Zero.

Caller: What? Did you say zero?

Me: They make the client pay it.

Caller: That's not how it works.

Me: It seems to work just fine.

Caller: No they are not allowed to charge the debtor more than what is owed.

Me: Says who?

Caller: That's how it works.

Me: Sure if you wish to wait months or years to get paid. I need people to pay faster.

Caller: And may I ask what this company is called?

Me: Hmm…not sure…but the three guys that collect for me are called "Left Hand" Luke, Vinnie "One Nut" and Jerry "The Gerbil".

Caller: Sounds hinky.

Me: Did you say kinky?
Caller: Hinky…as in weird.

Me: Oh, okay I heard it both ways then.

Caller: Sounds like you are using unscrupulous people.

Me: And that is different than you how?

Caller: We get results.

Me: Not as fast as the people I use.

Caller: They are doing some shady stuff.

Me: You don't even know them.

Caller: Do they use threatening tones or carry weapons?

Me: Now come to think about it they seem to like baseball a great deal…each one carries a bat.

Caller: I knew it…you are working with shysters.

Me: Well, what's your track record? How long does it take to recover bad debt.

Caller: Depends…could take weeks, could take months.

Me: That's too long, I'll stick to the guys who like to carry the bats.

Caller: You're be sorry.

Me: I'm already sorry this conversation lasted more than a minute.

Caller: What you're doing is wrong.

Me: Oh, but it feels so right.

Caller: You will get in trouble.

Me: Sounds like you are jealous.

Caller: Sir, I'm trying to help you.

Me: By trying to convince me to go with your service that takes way too long to collect anything and where I have to probably pay you a fee.

Caller: Yes we do charge for our services - 25-33% - but we don't use intimation or violence to collect.

Me: Well, if you did, your results would be so much better.

Caller: No Sir, we would get into trouble.

Me: Well it sounds like your service is poop.

Caller: Sir, you're poop.

Me: Pfft, my poop would do a better job collecting than your service.
{wait for it...}

Caller: You f**ker, you wasted my time.

Me: Bwahahahaha.

{Pfft, he hung up while I was laughing.}

Note: I would never encourage anyone to resort to violence when trying to collect a debt, however resorting to sarcasm when dealing with so-called debt recovery people is fair game.

Chapter 4

It's What I Do

"And I do it so well, don't ya think?"

The Quote Was High

Phone rings... it's a potential client who I sent a quote to a month ago.

{I already know how this will go...and it didn't disappoint}

Me: Hi J {name withheld to protect the guilty or in this case the utterly stupid}

J: Hey Rob, we'd love for you to work with us but your quote is high.

Me: Is it?

J: Yes, it's quite high.

Me: I'm sorry I told the quote to stop doing drugs.

J: Are you trying to be funny?

Me: Yup.

J: Well, I don't find it funny at all.

Me: Not even a little?

J: Are you going to be serious?

Me: I was being serious when I sent the quote.

J: But it's too high.

Me: {Me snickering} There you go again.

J: It's not funny.

Me: It kind of is.

J: Look we wanted you to give us a serious quote and now you are laughing at us.

Me: It was a serious quote, and you accused it of being high, so here I am laughing.

J: Yeah, I don't think it's going to work out.

Me: Well I could always send the quote to detox.

{Pfft, he hung up.}

Note: We (as entrepreneurs) all have our own methods of coming up with a price. However you determine your price and that's the price you stick with. As I've stated in several books, "The lower the price, the more hassles involved". The client wanted a lower price and was already demonstrating how much of a hassle they would be, so it's good to get rid of them quickly. Or in my case, share their story as a sarcastic teachable moment. Because that's what I do.

My Boss Wants A Quote

"Hey Rob, I love your books and really want my company to hire you."
{Message through Facebook}

Me: Great, now what's stopping them.

Them: They are currently using another marketing company for their SEO and Social Media.

{shares with me the website and social pages}

Me: Oy, not good.

Them: They have zero engagement on Facebook.

Me: I see that. The last 35 posts have received no likes, no comments and no shares.

Them: Can you give a quote?

Me: I can, but if you're not the decision maker then I'll just be wasting my time writing up a quote.

Them: Well ultimately my boss will make the decision. And the current agency is really cheap. So unless you are competitive I doubt he will budge.

Me: I'm not competitive. But, the results I generate will more than make up for my fee. Right now he's just throwing money away getting zip in return.

Them: I'll let him know.

Me: Not holding my breath.

Them: Do you NOT want the account?

Me: The question is not if I want the account, the question is will your boss being willing to pay my rate. And being that he'd rather pay for cheap and not results already speaks volumes.

{2 hours later}

Them: My boss wants a quote.

{I send a quote detailing my service}

{10 minutes go by}

Them: My boss says your price is too high and can you match the other company's price.

Me: No.

Them: But I really want you to work for us, the other company is horrible.

Me: Then tell your boss to stop being cheap.

Them: I don't want to get fired.

Me: I don't want to work with cheap people.

Them: Please.

Me: Well since you said please... it's still a NO.

Them: I don't understand.

Me: No is the opposite of Yes.

Them: I know that...just don't understand why you can't help us.

Me: Well if this conversation is any indication of what I will experience working for your company - no thank you.

Them: I think you'll regret not working for us.

Me: I already regret this chat happening.

{And I got blocked}

Note: I hate sending quotes when I know darn well how it will end. To me it's a giant time suck and a huge PITA. But the stories, oh the stories...yup, priceless.

Chapter 5

Being Sociable...Sort Of!

"It's a wonder I even have friends."

It's None Of Your Darn Business

Hey Rob my client is going with another social media service.
{Message received from a referral who really wanted us to take over}

Me: Okay. This is the first I'm hearing about it.

Them: Here's who they are using {gives link to FB page}

Me: OMG - that page has made just 6 posts this year and no posts the prior year. And he's hiring these people?

Them: Apparently so.

Me: Let me guess, they're cheap?

Them: Yep.

Me: Well, good luck to them.

Them: Looks like they made another post while we've been chatting.

Me: Okay 7 posts then. Which would be okay if this was the 7th day of the year, but being that we are close to the end of the year...their strategy is horrible.

Them: So not good?

Me: Nope.

Them: Should I tell them.

Me: Nope.

Them: Well, they really need your help.

Me: Yes, they do.

Them: So you do or don't want to help them?

Me: Yes, they need my help. No, they can't afford my help. And honestly, I don't really want to help them.

Them: Oh, okay. So not worth your time.

Me: Nope.

Them: Okay.

{10 minutes later receive an email from said client who hired the cheap social media company}

Client: Who I hire is none of your darn business. They are friends and I trust them.

Me: Your friend made it his business to help you. And he reached out to me. I don't want your business. Never did. But being that your trusted social media friend has only posted to their Facebook page 7x this whole year tells me all I need to know about their service.

{and my email bounced back as non-deliverable}

Note: Say no to PITA's (pain in the asses) early.

YouTube Is Not For Whippersnappers

Hey Man, That's Outdated Advice.
{Message received through YouTube regarding one of my videos}

Me: Well, I made that video almost 10 years ago.

Them: You should remove it.

Me: Why?

Them: As you said you made it almost 10 years ago, it's old.

Me: And?

Them: Dude, the information is not correct.

Me: Okay, so why don't you make a video with the correct information then?

Them: I don't make YouTube videos, YouTube is for old people.

Me: And yet here you are, viewing old videos.

Them: Dude, you need to get with the program, TikTok is where it's at.

Me: What's your TikTok channel and I'll look at your videos?

Them: I'm not sharing my TikTok, I don't want you looking at my videos.

Me: So if TikTok is all that, why are you here on YouTube?

Them: I'm getting ideas.

Me: Can't you get ideas on TikTok?

Them: People on YouTube explain things better, the videos are longer.

Me: Yup, now you're learning my young grasshopper.

Them: You seem confused. I'm not a grasshopper.

Me: It's an expression us older, more knowledgeable people say to whippersnappers like you when they are learning something new.

Them: What are you like 100 years old?

Me: That's why I'm on YouTube.

Note: If you go to a particular place (such as YouTube) for information, ideas or reference, then that's a good indication where you want to spend your time. Just saying. Why knock on the place you are getting your ideas from when could actually become part of that community and make a go of it? Something to ponder.

Show Me The Money

Five minutes after accepting this connection on LinkedIn...

Them: Briefly about our software - it automates LinkedIn + email outreach process. What you get: You receive qualified warm leads, interested in demo-call with you\your team members. How it works: AI searches for candidates you need, using attributes you put in the campaign. It builds a personalized dialog between AI and your potential customer, using the customer's personal data it can reach (Name of prospect's company, his\her position in this company, location etc.) The booked meeting is a result of this dialog. The main benefit You get extra 2-3 meetings daily without any actions - more potential customers and successful deals. Could software of this kind potentially fit into your business processes? If you think it could - let's book a meeting with our team. Here's the link: {URL removed}

Me: I get offers like yours 100x a day. If I scheduled a meeting with each and every one of them, I would never get anything done. So here's the deal...I will gladly schedule a call, but my time is super valuable. That being said...if you truly believe that your product can make me money - then you have to show me the money first. Yup, I will invoice you $750 and once you pay, I will gladly schedule a 20 minute time slot to hear your offer. Let me know where I can send the invoice so we can get started.

{And I got unfriended and blocked}

He Found Me, Then Blocked Me

Hi Rob,

I found your profile in the {name removed} Group on LinkedIn, and was wondering if you ever considered having a sales letter for your business.

This sales letter has generated 1,021 qualified sales appointments over the past 4+ years: {lists his URL}

- Made our company hundreds of thousands of dollars.
- Helped me get new referrals.
- Generated business partnerships.
- Gives me repeatable clientele.

And it continues to work!

Did you want me to write one for you?

Here's Who This is For:

1. You have a proven business with active clients.
2. You are in a B2B market.
3. You're open and willing to follow directions :)

That's it!

If that's you, I'd be happy to write a sales letter for you that generates more sales calls, brings in more clientele, and significantly increases your sales.

If that interests you...

Just hit reply, and let me know.

First come, first serve.

Thanks for reading :)

Steve

ps. If you're not interested, that's ok too. You're still awesome in my books, no matter what anyone else says :-)

Me: I need to remove myself from that group…all I get is spam messages from people thinking they can help me when they have no clue what I do.

{I get unfriended and blocked}

Note: A simple "Hi, love what you're doing, let's chat sometime", works so much better than sending out some long winded pitch…but hey some guru is getting rich teaching the masses how to be morons.

You Need Something Alright

I read a Facebook post.
Then left a reply.
Then it dawns on me the person has no sense of humor and won't find my reply funny.
So I immediately erase my reply.

{1.2 milliseconds later}

I get a direct message from the person who wrote the post saying the comment was not funny.

Me: That's why I deleted it.

Them: Well I saw it, and didn't find it funny.

Me: For $49.95 I'll sell you a sense of humor.

Them: I don't need one.

Me: You need something alright.

Them: What's that supposed to mean.

Me: Means you're too serious. You need to lighten up.

Them: How did we even become connections?

Me: You reached out and friend requested me.

Them: Why would I do that?

Me: The universe thought you needed humor in your life.

Them: I don't believe in all that mumbo-jumbo the universe controls everything. I control my own destiny.

Me: But do you really?

Them: Yes, everything I do is under my control.

Me: Like this conversation.

Them: Yes, I'm in control.

Me: If you say so.

Them: Why are you bothering me?

Me: You initiated this conversation, so it is you bothering me.

Them: No you commented on a post with your ridiculous sarcasm.

Me: And I deleted it immediately after because I knew you wouldn't get it.

Them: It wasn't funny.

Me: It was hilarious to those with a sense of humor.

Them: I didn't find it funny at all.

Me: Yup, and it was deleted.

Them: It wasn't funny.

Me: Sure I can't sell you a sense of humor?

Them: No, I don't need it.

Me: How about my new "I let people control me, even though I control my own destiny" course? It's only $99 and it comes with the sense of humor package for free.

{Wait for it...}

Them: F You.

{And I got unfriended and blocked}

Note: I was thinking of sending this humorless excuse for a human a few of my "Rob Versus" books...but I'm sure he would be so triggered by them, I'd be sued for mental anguish...oh, but it would be so worth it.

Retired And Blocked

Grr...for those that read my posts you know I have a love/hate relationship with LinkedIn.

Well yesterday I sent a friend request to what I hoped would be a new connection. And instead of this person accepting, I receive a direct message...

Them: I'm retired and no longer accepting connections or actively using this account.

Me: Okay, then why not have your profile reflect that.

Them: What I do, and how I do it is my business.

Me: Yes of course it is...it would be silly for me to tell you how to do things the proper way.

Them: You seem arrogant, I'm glad I didn't accept your connection.

Me: Why would you? You're retired and not actively using your account.

Them: What is your problem?

Me: Well since you asked... I seem to have a low iron count, elevated blood pressure, slight bruise on my hip and I got dirt on my sneakers this morning.

Them: I'm retired I don't need this.

Me: Then change your profile to reflect that.

Them: I'm reporting you.

Me: Why?

Them: You're bothering me.

Me: You didn't have to respond to my connection request. You could have just rejected it and not sent me a message.

Them: Stop sending me messages.

Me: Right, you're retired.

Them: Exactly.

Me: So you have plenty of time to argue with me then?

{Apparently not as I got blocked}

Note: Do I even need to add a note here? Isn't this one self-explanatory? Seriously, if you're retired and don't want to be bothered, why are you even on social media?

Bugger Off

So I reached out to someone on LinkedIn as we have many mutual friends.
I receive...

"Thank you very much for reaching out to me. Given the large number of talented people I have worked with and for during my lengthy career I take a conservative approach to social networking except for commercial purposes and only link to those individuals I know well. I hope you understand my perspective and that our paths cross in the future so we can get to know each other."

So I reply...

"Being that's what social media is all about...crossing paths and all...I would think a person of your caliber would be more willing to accept someone who has a lot of mutual friends and can add to your expanding network. Or is what you are saying just a fancy way of saying "bugger off"?

{Guess I will never know the answer, he blocked me}

Note: Yup, I've embraced the fact that "How to win friends and influence people" is not something I'm known for, wouldn't you agree?

Oh Yeah…Could Be!

Hey Rob send us your resume.
{Message drops in my LinkedIn inbox from a non-connection}

Me: Why?

Them: We love what you are doing and want to consider hiring you.

Me: Hiring me for what?

Them: Send us your resume and we will gladly discuss it further.

Me: I'll pass.

Them: It could be a very worthwhile proposition.

Me: The key phrase being "could be".

Them: Look we feel you would make a great candidate for the position.

Me: For which you haven't told me anything about it.

Them: Send us your resume and we'd be glad to tell you all about it.

Me: I stopped using a resume was when I was 25 years old, that was almost 28 years ago.

Them: Well we require a resume.

Me: Okay well you can either tell me more about the position or jump in a time machine and go back to when I last used a resume.

Them: So you aren't going to send us a resume then?

Me: Well let's put it this way...you'd have a better chance of finding a time machine and traveling back to when I was 25 then me sending you my resume in the present time.

Them: You don't know what you are passing up.

Me: That's right I don't know...but if it requires me sending you something I haven't used in 28 years that you can learn just from reading my LinkedIn profile then I'll pass.

{And I got blocked}

Note: I'm not even sure why people even use resumes anymore when you can list all your education, work history, publications and more directly to LinkedIn. But I guess having all that information on a piece of paper looks cool.

Pfft...He Wasn't Civil!

Sometimes I respond to posts on Facebook...which then go sideways fast. This one...oh yeah, didn't disappoint.

Michael V posted: While I believe in Freedom of Speech, I also believe in civility.

Me: If my freedom of speech makes you feel uncivil that's on you not me.

{So Michael V deletes my comment then adds...}

Michael V: I removed the comments from some guy who seems to always write seemingly fictitious stories about people who persistently want to hire him while he resists. They keep bugging, but he says no. I can't count how many times he has posted stuff like that. He might do better writing fiction novels instead of self-help knockoffs.

Me: Fictitious? Nope. But thanks for reading.

{And I got blocked}

Note: Hahaha...it's so nice when people talk about me after erasing my comment "if my freedom of speech makes you feel uncivil that's on you not me". And he proved my point. He allowed his emotions to dictate how civil he was. And he got himself a spot in this awesome book.

Invited Then Blocked

Hey Rob, come join my Facebook group.
{Message received after accepting a new connection as a friend}

Me: Why?

Them: I think you'll like what we are doing.

Me: {So I accept the offer to join, look at his group and then I notice something strange}
Hey, I see you haven't posted to your group in months.

Them: Yeah, not much going on right now, but soon.

Me: How soon?

Them: Whenever we post you'll know.

Me: {Removing myself from the group}
Nah, I'm done.

Them: Why did you leave?

Me: You said I would like what you were doing, I didn't, so I left.

Them: Seems rude.

Me: Rude is connecting with someone, then inviting them to a group that has zero activity, then getting mad when they leave.

Them: You're a jerk.

Me: Oh yes, it's my fault. At least in my groups, which by the way you will never be a member, I post to every day.

Them: I only post when I need to be heard.

Me: Awesome, can you also block me so I never see your profile again.

{And he did}

Note: Ugh, whomever is teaching this madness needs kicked in the jimmies. Why send invites out to a group page that you don't even post to? At least post some worthwhile content before inviting people.

Hello LinkedIn Loser…Goodbye!

Cheryl: Hey Rob, I really appreciate your connecting and I'd love to see if there are some ways to collaborate and refer some business.

I would love to hear more about your business and share 2 ways we are helping clients;

1) I assist entrepreneurs with 2 to 5 appointments per day with your targeted/ideal clients with systems and Virtual Assistants.

2) I can possibly get you (or your clients) a big chunk of cash for your company (stimulus money) that you don't have to repay.

If you are open to it, let's set a time to speak for a few minutes and say hello. Please use my calendar link to select a good day and time to meet with my CEO and I - {url removed}

LOL no sales pitch, just looking to connect and help firms in our ever changing world.

Me: Not sure why I need to schedule on someone's calendar just to say hello, I can do that right here and save myself considerable time. Now if you want to know more about me the first thing I recommend is to read my profile.

And seriously why do you assume most companies need 2-5 appointments per day? If I had that many, I wouldn't get anything done. The way I have my business structured that makes me maximum results only requires 2-5 appointments per month.

Note: Grr! Who is teaching people this gawd-awful method of inbox sales dumping? You pitch me, then end it with LOL no sales pitch.

Chapter 6

Life Choices

"Yeah, I choose sarcasm!"

Split Personality

Phone rings…Caller ID Displays "Ntl Security"

Me: Hello.

Caller 1: May I speak to Ann?
{he says in broken English}

Me: {I knew right then it was a scam, but decided to play along} Speaking!

Caller 1: Hmm, uh, okay. Ann have you received your new Medicare card for 2022?

Me: No, I haven't received it.

Caller 1: Is your name Ann Stafford of {gives address about 30 miles away}.

Me: No, I moved.

Caller 1: Oh, okay…I will need to transfer you to my superwisor.

Me: Okay transfer away.

Caller 2: Is this Ann?
{she says in a much clearer English accent}

Me: YUP!

Caller 2: Have you received your new Medicare card for 2022?

Me: NOPE!

Caller 2: When do you suppose you will receive it?

Me: Well by my watch, it looks like it might arrive by 3pm on a Tuesday.

Caller 2: Sir…Ann…that's not how it works.

Me: Oh…then I have no idea when it will arrive.

Caller 2: Am I talking to Anne Stafford of {repeats address that Caller 1 gave}

Me: YUP.

Caller 2: Ann is a woman's name.

Me: And?

Caller 2: But you sound like a man.

Me: And? Have I questioned your life choices?

Caller 2: Uh, well… it looks like you aren't the primary person on the account so I can't proceed.

Me: Who do you have listed as primary?

Caller 2: A Jim Stafford…is he available?

Me: That's me too. I go by both names.

Caller 2: What? I don't understand.

Me: I have a split personality - sometimes Ann, sometimes Jim…sometimes this guy named Rob Anspach.

Caller 2: You bastard…you wasted our time again.

Me: Bwahahahaha.

Note: If the service calling doesn't match the Caller ID it's most likely a scam. And sadly, these nefarious actors prey on Medicare recipients in hopes of gleaning their financial information or using the Medicare information for unscrupulous activities. Don't give any information out, just waste their time on the call.

Medicare You Say

Phone rings… Caller ID displays St Joseph Hospital

{But our local St. Joseph Hospital closed years ago, so yeah a scam}

Me: Hello.

{I can hear music playing, so I say louder…}

Me: Hello.

Caller: Oh Hello Sir, this is Jennifer from the Medicare Department.

Me: Medicare you say…okay.

Jennifer: Yes, Sir. Have you received your new Medicare card?

Me: You know…I don't ever recall receiving one.

Jennifer: Okay, can you tell me your date of birth.

Me: You called me, don't you have that information?

Jennifer: Yes Sir, we are just double checking.

Me: Hmm, so you're calling to make sure that your information is correct?

Jennifer: That's right Sir.

Me: Okay…let's start with my name. What do your records say my name is?

Jennifer: S-T-A-F-F-O-R-D

Me: {Not my last name but somehow these scammers think I'm this Stafford guy} Yeah, but the second F in my name is silent, so you don't need to spell it.

Jennifer: Sir, I don't understand. Is Stafford your name or not?

Me: It's the name I'm associated with.

Jennifer: Okay let's proceed.

Me: To where?

Jennifer: Sir? You still with me?

Me: Sorry, I was thinking about waterboarding myself.

Jennifer: Sir, I'm not sure what you said, but can you get your Medicare number I will wait.

Me: It's not on me.

Jennifer: That's okay I can wait while you get it.

Me: Okay, you'll be waiting a long time then.

Jennifer: Why is that Sir?

Me: I haven't been sent a card yet?

Jennifer: Do you know when you should receive it?

Me: Well let's see, according to my watch…in about 13 years.

Jennifer: Okay, we will call you every day to remind you.

Me: Yup, thought so.

{and she hung up}

Note: The deal is they have no idea who has Medicare and who doesn't. They use an auto-dialer to call a list of numbers and when someone answers they go into the script. But as I've said before, never ever give a stranger your information.

Just Wanting To Argue

Phone rings...caller ID displays "Scam"
{I answer it anyway}

Me: Hello.

Prerecorded message plays... "Press 1 to learn how to get discounted affordable health insurance."

{So I press 1}

Them: Hi this is Chris with discounted health insurance how can I help you?

Me: Do you mean how can you help me with insurance or with anything in general. Because I have a lot of questions.

Them: Do you have questions about health insurance?

Me: Not really.

Them: Sir, can I ask your age?

Me: Sure.

Them: {Slight pause} Oh, okay, how old are you?

Me: Probably older than you.

Them: Can you give me an exact age?

Me: How old do you think I am?

Them: I don't know, that's why I'm asking.

Me: What other questions do you have? Maybe I can answer those first.

Them: No, that's not how it works. I can't skip over the questions. I need you to answer them so I can fill in the form and then we can address the next questions.

Me: Seriously?

Them: Yes, that's how I was trained. I can't skipped questions.

Me: Okay, let me ask you a question before you continue asking me more questions. What if I don't find your prices affordable?

Them: Sir, we offer discounted affordable prices, everyone can afford our health insurance.

Me: Well, if I can't afford it, then it's not affordable.

Them: Sir, can I proceed with more questions?

Me: Will the next question be would you like to know how much it is?

Them: No, what is your age?

Me: We have already gone over that question.

Them: You didn't answer it.

Me: Yes I did.

Them: No you didn't. And I believe you are wasting my time.

Me: Really? You called me. Now you are saying I'm wasting your time.

Them: Sir, you have no intention of giving me your information or buying health insurance, you just want to argue.

Me: No, I don't.

Them: Yes, you do.

Me: Nope.

Them: Yes.

Me: Okay, maybe you're right.

Them: Of course I'm right.

Me: Actually I just wanted to see how long I could keep you on the phone and prevent you from scamming others.

Them: You a-hole.

Me: Maybe next time you won't call me then.

{wait for it...}

Them: F-You

Never Gonna Happen!

My mobile rings…Caller ID displays "Toothsmiths"
{I have no dealings with such company, so yeah must be a scam…and it was}

Me: Hello.

Caller: Hi Sir, this is Sam with National Benefits calling to see if you received the updated medical card?
{he says in a deep accent}

Me: Nope haven't received it. But let me ask you why did my Caller ID says Toothsmiths and not whatever it is you call your company of the moment?

Sam: We use a rotating series of numbers to help us connect better with the people that need us.

Me: But do they really need you?

Sam: Every person on Medicare needs our service.

Me: And you think I qualify then?

Sam: What is your Medicare number?

Me: No idea.

Sam: I can wait while you find it.

Me: Okay give me a few minutes.

{I walk around the house for about 5 minutes opening and closing doors and rummaging through boxes}

Me: You know I just can't seem to find it.

Sam: Okay Sir, we can try it another way… what is your social security number?

Me: You know Sam we really don't know each other that well, so I don't feel comfortable giving you that information.

Sam: You can trust me.

Me: How about you give me your social security number first as a sign of good faith then?

Sam: Sir, that's not how it works.

Me: Sure it is…you give me yours, and I'll give you mine.

Sam: Fine Sir… {rattles off 9 digits, most likely someone else's Social Security numbers}

Me: See that wasn't too hard now was it?

Sam: Now you Sir, may I have your Social Security numbers?

Me: Hell no, my momma didn't raise no fool.

Sam: You Mother F-er.

Me: Sam you need to settle down and not get so angry.

{Sam is now screaming at me in some foreign language}

{in the background I can hear "just hang up, just hang up, we will get him eventually"}

Me: Hahahahaha.

Sam: A-Hole

{and he hung up}

Note: Never give out your social security numbers over the phone to someone you don't know. Heck even in person, if you don't know them, don't share. It's a simple concept…yet, many fail simplicity. Just the other day I was in Costco and I overheard a customer sharing her social security and credit card information over the phone while shopping. Then people wonder how they got their identity compromised.

Chapter 7

He Who Shall Be Named

"And named he was!"

Voldemort For The Win

"Hey Rob I know a person who is hiring for a digital marketer, and I thought of you."
{Message received from a connection on Facebook whom I've never communicated with on chat before.}

Me: You do know I own my own media company don't you?

Them: Yeah, but this person is a rockstar and is looking for a unicorn.

Me: Hmm...are they looking for a digital marketer or a unicorn?

Them: You're serious right?

Me: I try not to be.

Them: A unicorn is someone so unique that their very existence is mythical.

Me: Yeah...not interested.

Them: But you're so good at what you do.

Me: How would you know? Up until this moment you have never liked, commented or shared my posts and this is the first time you sent me a chat.

Them: I've been watching you.

Me: How creepy.

Them: Do you want me to refer you to my friend or not?

Me: Not if I have to be a Unicorn.

Them: But you are.

Me: No, I'm not. I'm more like Voldemort hunting down the Unicorn.

Them: Wow, I didn't expect you to say that.

Me: Well, I didn't expect this conversation to last this long, but here we are.

Them: Yeah, you're right you're not a good fit for my friend.

Me: That's because I own a media company...and hunt down unicorns.

{And I got blocked}

Note: Yes, the title of the book was inspired by this conversation. And yes, meeting J.K. Rowling is on my bucket list. But I think the real question is, "which Hogwarts house do I belong in?"

The Guy With Many Questions

"Hey Rob your podcast is cool, I would like to be considered as a guest."
{message drops in my Facebook chat}

Me: {looking at the message but not replying}

Person: And here's a list of questions I would like you to ask me when I'm on your show. {lists 11 questions}

Me: That's now how I work.

Person: What do you mean?

Me: I never use questions people suggest.

Person: But how will you know what to ask me?

Me: I've done over 200 interviews, and have never once used a question or list of questions someone supplied to me.

Person: But I'm different.

Me: You sure are.

Person: What's that supposed to mean?

Me: You're a mythical creature that thinks they are so special.

Person: I do not, I just think that if I'm on your show you should ask me questions I'm familiar with.

Me: Not going to happen.

Person: I don't see what is wrong with giving you questions in advance.

Me: Yet the over 200 guests before you never requested such silliness. They knew their material, they knew that no matter what I asked they were prepared with an answer.

Person: Well I like to know the questions.

Me: Again, not going to happen.

Person: I don't understand.

Me: Okay, from the beginning…you requested to be on my podcast, then presented a list of dumb questions, followed by me saying NO, you didn't like my answer, then you tried to convince me you are different, I retorted that you're mythical and you rejected that assessment but still insisted I use your questions to which I said not going to happen again. You clear on the understanding part?

{wait for it…}

Person: You're such a dumbf**k

Me: And yet, I don't need a list of questions to make an interview sound awesome.

Person: I rescind my offer to be a guest on your podcast, I don't think it would've been worth my time.

Me: You sure… we could have called the episode "Rob Versus The Guy with Many Questions".

{Pfft…he blocked me}

Note: On my E-Heroes Podcast website I have this…

A Message To PR Firms & Those Wanting To Be On This Podcast:

I don't accept unsolicited requests to be on my podcast. The only way to appear on my podcast is if:

(1) I send a personal invite or

(2) someone that's been on the podcast suggests I reach out.

Oh there's a lot more, but the gist is I'm selective of who comes on the show and it has to be on my terms.

Chapter 8

This Is The Sci-Fi Chapter

"Because why not?"

All Too Easy

Phone rings...Caller ID displays "Scam Likely"

{But the force compelled me to answer...and answer I did.}

Me: Hello.

Caller: Is this Annie?

Me: That is a name I once used?

Caller: Huh, hmm...do you live on {gives a street name 50 miles away}?

Me: No, I moved to Mustafar

Caller: Our records don't show that.

Me: I find your lack of record keeping disturbing.

Caller: Your last name is Stafford, correct?

Me: Well it does start with an S but not Stafford.

Caller: Can you update me with your full name.

Me: Skywalker...Annie is short for Anakin.

Caller: Why are you wasting my time?

Me: One day I will be the best Jedi ever. I will even learn how to stop people from scam calling others.

Caller: F-You.

Me: No, the saying is "May The Force Be With You"

Caller: F-You.

Me: All too easy.

Caller: Dumb A-hole.

Me: Most impressive, Obi-Wan has taught you well.

Caller: Hang up and stop wasting my time.

Me: You are beaten. It is useless to resist.

{pfft, he hung up}

Note: It's always fun to just use random lines from Star Wars movies, sometimes it works…sometimes they catch on and sometimes it's just funny has heck.

Long Live Flash

The Department of Education called with a message regarding forbearance of my student loans and I should press 5 to speak to an agent.

{So I did}

Me: Hello.

Agent: This is Sam Jones, how may I help you?

Me: Sam Jones you say, hmm.

Agent: Is there a problem?

Me: Can you say "Ming is a psycho"?

Agent: What? I don't understand.

Me: Well, you're Sam Jones right?

Agent: Yes.

Me: Well, Sam Jones played Flash Gordon in the 1980 sci-fi movie.

Agent: Who?

Me: You know... "Flash Gordon, Quarterback, New York Jets".

Agent: What are you talking about?

Me: Flash... aaaaaahaaaaa... Savior of the Universe.

Agent: Sir, that's not me.

Me: Of course not, you're just a scammer.

Agent: {curses at me in some foreign language}

Me: Long Live Flash!

{Pfft...he hung up}

Note: My generation had all the good movies to reference. What? You've never watched Flash Gordon? Are you on the right pills? Pfft, it's an iconic science fiction movie that incorporates music from the rock band Queen. Yeah...it's a must see. Now go watch it.

It's The Sarcasm's Fault

"Hey Rob you're sarcasm doesn't work on me."
{Message received thru FB chat}

Me: Okay Jedi.

Them: I'm not a Jedi.

Me: Hmm, well I can picture you waving your hand every time you reply to me.

Them: That's crazy.

Me: Yeah, but totally true.

Them: You do know that sarcasm is the lowest form of wit, right?

Me: And it's the highest form of intelligence too.

Them: You're wrong.

Me: Am I?

Them: Yes.

Me: Look it up Jedi.

Them: Stop calling me that.

Me: Why?

Them: I don't wave my hands when I reply to you, that's why.

Me: You don't wave your hands when you reply to me?

Them: No I don't!

Me: Okay Jedi, I believe you.

Them: You do?

Me: Nah, but I bet I'm making you angry, right?

Them: Why are you like this?

Me: I blame it on the sarcasm, it's affected every ounce of my being. Doctors say I have at most another 45 years to live.

Them: Really?

Me: No, I'm being sarcastic.

Them: You're stupid.

Me: Hahaha, that was just too easy.

Them: I hate you.

Me: I know.

Note: Mystical religions are no match for my sarcasm.

Chapter 9

Saturday Shenanigans

"Sarcasm doesn't take weekends off."

Grilled Sarcasm

So I received this email on a Saturday afternoon...and the way it was written I just had to respond.

And so I did.

It's how I roll.

It's just not what they expected.

Here's how it went down...

Congrats on making it to the end of the day.

Me: I didn't know we were congratulating people now. Do I win something? A gold sticker? But seriously, I received this email at 2pm on a Saturday, so is that now considered the end of the day? What about the 10 hours that are between 2pm and midnight? Are they not considered in the equation?

It's been a rough one, huh?

Me: No, not really. I actually got to relax a bit today.

You're trying to figure out how to best market your business, but you've got so much on your plate that it's hard to get a handle on it.

Me: The only thing that was on my plate was a grilled cheese and some potato chips.

I hear ya. That's why I'm here: I've got some tips for marketing your business that might make things easier!

Me: There is nothing easier than grilled cheese...well maybe Ramon Noodles.

First, think about what your customers value. What do they want most from your product/service? It's important to identify their main priorities so that you can make sure to address them in your message.

Me: It's a Saturday. I don't want to think about customers now, can we get back to my grilled cheese...mmm.

Second, think about how your business can help meet those priorities. How does it serve the needs of your customer base? If you're still not sure, ask a few customers! Find out what they like most about working with you—and what they like least.

Me: It's my lovely sarcasm, they just adore it.

Third, bring it all together by weaving those themes into an engaging marketing message. You want your message to be concise, but also take the time to highlight exactly why someone should choose you over another company or product. You don't have to overcomplicate it, but make sure to take the time to get it right!

Me: Okay weaving it together and I have grilled sarcasm...woot, woot.

Taking the time to answer these questions will be crucial for finding the right marketing message for your business. And if you want to learn more about how we can help with this process, just let us know!

Me: How's your quick wit and sarcastic timing? If you want to help me you have to keep up with the sarcasm.

I don't think they appreciated my answers as I received back, *"We are removing you from our list."*

Note: I get hundreds of emails a day and 99.99% of them are junk…absolute garbage…but it's that .01% that bring joy to my life by being so ridiculous that I have to respond.

Yeah, I'm The Imposter

Phone rings it's 5:45pm on Saturday...caller ID displays a California number.
{I answer it and hear...}

Hi, you called me and I'm returning your call. Yeah I'm just... {The guy sounds drunk & confused}

Me: Who are you?

Caller: Well who are you?

Me: Not sure what you want but most scammers usually start off with an agenda.

Caller: I'm not a scammer, but I could use $144,000 and you called me.

Me: I never called you.

Caller: Yes you did, my caller ID says so.

Me: What number did I call you on?

Caller: {Shares one of my numbers}

Me: Well that is one of my numbers, but it's for incoming calls only, I can't make outgoing calls on that number.

Caller: Well someone called me from that number.

Me: It was probably spoofed. Did someone leave a message?

Caller: No, but why did someone call me on your number?

Me: I have no idea why they called.

Caller: Well we follow each other on Facebook.

Me: Okay, what's your name.

Caller: {Gives name, but it didn't make sense the way it was pronounced}

Me: Say what?

Caller: Well I have lots of profiles.

Me: Whatever floats your boat I suppose.

Caller: Yeah, you commented on one of my posts.

Me: I think I would remember.

Caller: Yes you did.

Me: You mentioned $144,000 why do you need that amount?

Caller: For Thanksgiving. I want to feed the community.

Me: And what community would that be?

Caller: My community.

Me: Yes and you live where?

Caller: In California.

Me: So you want to feed all of California?

Caller: No just me and my closest friends.

Me: I'll pass.

Caller: But we are friends on Facebook.

Me: I doubt it.

Caller: Okay, well I'd like to be your friend.

Me: Doubt it again.

Caller: Can you tell me more about you? Tell me your name and what you do.

Me: I thought you said we are friends on Facebook.

Caller: Well, I need to see if you are the person I'm friends with or someone impersonating my friend.

Me: I'm definitely an imposter.

Caller: Well, okay can you not call me then.

{And he hung up}

Note: Yeah…I admit, I get the weirdest calls.

Chapter 10

Attitude Adjustments Needed

"The power of my sarcasm will save you…bwahahaha!"

Arrogant & Cocky

"Hey Rob, I didn't know you did all that!"

{A response I received thru Facebook chat from someone who visited my website}

Me: Yup.

Them: How long have you been doing that?

Me: Over 20 years.

Them: Really?

Me: Yup.

Them: But didn't I meet you in 1998 in Arizona at a marketing convention?

Me: Yup, sold that previous company in 2014, but I started the media company in 2001 and ran both for about 13 years.

Them: Oh, okay.

Me: Do you need my help or were you just curious?

Them: Just curious I suppose.

Me: Okay...hey what are you doing now?

Them: Kind of struggling. My business went under. I'm facing bankruptcy.

Me: Wow, sorry.

Them: Yeah for me, the marketing just didn't pan out the way it did for you. You got the success and I didn't.

Me: Marketing is just a small part of my success. Attitude is the major part. I always found a way to keep going. And never felt that someone else was more successful than I was.

Them: You sound arrogant...why do all the cocky people get all the success?

{Pfft, I was then blocked from responding}

Note: Maybe I am a bit arrogant and cocky...but then again, I never gave up on my dreams. I work hard every day to make sure that I am always moving forward in a positive way. Were there hard times? You bet. But, I never lost sight of my goals.

The Postal Rules

Sent a package via USPS to a client in California.

After 2 weeks the client notified me they hadn't received it.

So I tracked the package - it was sitting in a USPS transfer station about 10 miles away from client.

Another 7 days go by and the package is still sitting in that transfer station.

So I sent the client another package which they received 3 days later.

So now it's 60 days later - I go to my local post office and they have the first package I sent.

Apparently it was sent back as the California postal people couldn't deliver it.

But here's the kicker...my local post office now wants me to pay $$ to accept it back.

Me: Nah, keep it.

USPS Clerk: No, you have to pay to accept it back.

Me: I don't want it back. I paid for it to be delivered, which apparently wasn't done.

USPS Clerk: Your customer didn't pick it up.

Me: I put the customer's exact address on it so it should have gone to his house.

USPS Clerk: It didn't for some unknown reason, so they required him to pick it up.

Me: So basically they were too lazy to deliver it.

USPS Clerk: No idea. You're going to have to pay to accept it back.

Me: Nope.

USPS Clerk: Fine, just take it, but next time we will need to charge you.

Me: If you say so.

USPS Clerk: It's the rules.

Me: Yeah, apparently they are one way rules and if I complain enough you won't charge me.

USPS Clerk: I'll remember for next time.

Me: Alrighty then.

Note: Packages get "lost" I understand that…but this is why tracking codes were added to shipping labels. And when customers can track a package and see it's stuck in some warehouse, don't blame the recipient for not picking it up when it clearly was an operational error. But I digress, there are still some world class workers at the USPS, just wish they all were.

Training Day

Stopped by the local mini-mart to grab an iced tea. I pay the cashier and then stand there waiting.

Clerk: Sir?

Me: Yes, can I get a receipt?

Clerk: Not sure how to do that.

Me: Let me guess today is your first day right?

Clerk: No, this is my third day.

Me: Well I believe printing receipts is covered in your training today.

Clerk: Not sure, let me get a Manager.

Me: Yes, go get the Manager.

Manager: Can I help you Sir?

Me: A receipt please.

Manager: Sorry, I'll get you a receipt right away. {Shows clerk how to print a receipt}

Me: See, now you're trained to print receipts.

Clerk: You are the only one in 3 days who has asked for a receipt.

Me: No, I'm the only one patient enough to have you trained the proper way.

Manager: I heard that.

Note: It's weird to me how many places no longer give customers receipts. How do you prove you purchased something if you didn't get a receipt? Or how do you return something without proof of purchase. Always ask for a receipt. Even if it means getting someone properly trained. Oh, and don't get me started on checking receipts at Walmart. {Inner voice saying: calm down Rob, just calm down} I'm okay. But thanks for being concerned. It was touch and go there, but I got it under control now. Anyhoos…get a receipt. That's all I got to say about that.

It's a Matter Of Urgency

Sent a new client an invoice to get started.

After 3 days no credit card payment had been received. So I emailed them...

Me: Hi, my team is in place and ready to go just waiting on you to pay.

Them: Oh, I sent your invoice to our accounts payable department when you sent it to me.

Me: Okay, and do they know we get paid upfront to start?

Them: Yes, I believe I told them to pay you right away.

{Five more days go by}

Me {reaching out again}: You've granted my team access to your digital assets, but we still haven't received payment.

Them: I contacted accounts payable and they mailed a check.

Me: When did they mail it?

Them: Same day I asked them.

Me: Just saying had they paid via a credit card, we would have started a week ago. Now we wait for a check (that may or may not have been mailed) and then wait for the bank to clear it.

Them: Well, you could have just started and had faith that we would pay you.

Me: That's not how we work. So until payment is received your project gets delayed.

Them: That doesn't seem fair. We can't make the postal service deliver the check faster.

Me: Using a credit card to get started would have solved this whole problem.

Them: Well, our accounts payable person only pays with a check.

Me: I would say if you want us to get started without further delays you pay via credit card and cancel the check.

Them: Not sure you understand...our accounts person only pays with a check.

Me: Then we wait.

Them: But we need you to get started right away.

Me: Apparently you didn't convey your urgency to your accounts payable person.

{3 hours later... received credit card payment}

Note: Client was huge PITA...who I fired after 20 days.

Chapter 11

If Only They Were Honest

"But would these stories be as a funny? I don't think so."

Nope

Phone rings - caller ID says Choice Electric.

Me: Hello.

Them: Bob?

Me: Hello.

Them: {They say again} Bob?

Me: Can I help you?

Them: This is Choice Electric the power generation partner with your electric service provider.

Me: Nope.

Them: Yes, we are.

Me: Nope.

Them: You like saying nope.

Me: What do you want?

Them: We are calling to tell you your 24 month commitment with us is almost up and it's time to renew.

Me: Nope.

Them: Yes.

Me: I know who my electric generation provider is and it's not you.

Them: Sure is.

Me: Hey frack off.

Them: You don't talk to me like that!

Me: Or what?

Them: I know where you live.

Me: I'll be waiting.

Them: We will call you again tomorrow.

Me: And my answer will still be nope.

{Pfft he hung up}

Note: This company is relentless, they have called dozens of times insisting I am a customer. Never was, never will be. These types of callers are aggressive and will try every trick in the book to get you to give them your information. Don't do it.

Not Yet

Did You Sign Up Yet?

{Was the recurring phrase I kept receiving from this person…and after saying no the third time things took a turn…but I'm getting ahead of the story…so let's catch you up, shall we?}

As I do for every new LinkedIn connection I send a short 15 second video thanking them for connecting and I include the transcript for those who don't want to or can't watch the video. Some reply, some don't. Some even, like the person below, have a lengthy conversation.

But this one seemed hinky from the start.

The person I connected with (I will call them JG) displayed on their profile as working as a Business Development Strategist for Disney and also involved with a crypto investment company.

Being that the first time they replied to my "Thanks For connecting" video was at 4am. Now you might be thinking 4am isn't odd if they are from another country, but their profile had Florida as their home base. Then 4 hours later they respond again. Oh yeah, now my Spidey-sense is tingling.

JG: (4:03 am) It's nice to have you also.
{not a common phrase said in the US}
JG: (8:17 am) Good Morning, Rob!
Me: (9:03 am) Good morning to you.

JG: (10:21 am) It's my pleasure.
JG: (10:35 am) How is your morning and hope you are having a great day.
Me: (11:13 am) Going good.
JG: (5:16 pm) Awesome. I see you write books, what's the title to your book so I can check it online.
Me: (5:24 pm) You can find all my books on Amazon at www.amazon.com/author/robertanspach
{Now pay attention to their next response}
JG: (5:32 pm) Can I get the books on Amazon?
{I had just stated where the person could go to get the books, ugh}
Me: (5:33 pm) Yes, the link I posted will take you right to my Amazon author page.
JG: (5:34 pm) Okay.
JG: (6:01 pm) You there?

{Then at 7:42pm I get a ping on my WhatsApp account}

JG: Hi Rob it's JG.
Me: Hi, I see you found me on WhatsApp.
JG: I hope you don't mind, I find WhatsApp more secure than LinkedIn.
Me: Okay.
JG: You going to meeting?
Me: No it's like 8pm here - is there something you need?
JG: Let's chat tomorrow.

{then the next day at 12:15 pm - my WhatsApp is pinging again}

JG: Hi Rob, how are you doing today?
Me: Good.

JG: I want to buy your book. How much is it sold for?
Me: They range from $3.99 for the kindle up to $24.95 for the print versions, depends on what books you want.
JG: Okay, it's cheap and affordable.
JG: I will purchase it.
Me: Which one did you buy?
JG: I am buying just two.
JG: Do you have knowledge on Crypto?
JG: Or have you ever invest in cryptocurrency
Me: Which ones did you buy?
JG: Rob Versus The Scammers and Rob Versus The Whackadoos.
Me: Awesome. As to your crypto question, my firm did the marketing for a crypto event years ago, but I have not personally invested in it.
JG: I am a senior account officer in Crypto company, we trade cryptocurrency for our investors in better rate and make better profit for them.
Me: Is there a website for your crypto company?
JG: Yes we have a company site to that.
JG: Always let me know when you write a new inspiring book.
Me: What's the site and I'll check it out.
JG: Ok.

{it's now about 2:30 pm}

JG: {Gives URL to the crypto site}
JG: Here is the link above.
JG: When you make an investment with any amount of money then you buy bitcoin with it with a bitcoin account you will create for yourself then I will help you trade it. When you sign up and your account is verified,

you are entitled to $50 on your account balance. After your three weeks of successful trading is completed and you withdraw your profit. You will also have to pay me 10% commission of your profit for helping you trade.
JG: Send me a screenshot if you have any challenge trying to register

{ 3 hours go by }

JG: Hey!
Me: Yes.
JG: Were you able to register with the link yet?
Me: No been busy all day.
JG: Oh, okay you working on new book?
Me: Well I am working on another book, but my firm creates marketing for companies all over the globe.
JG: What kind of marketing actually?
JG: Could you do a marketing for me also?
JG: For the Crypto?
JG: Are you there?
JG: I guess you are busy at the moment.
Me: Calm your jets, I just set my phone down for a minute.
JG: How much do you charge for marketing?
Me: It depends on what you need exactly.
JG: I need social marketing that can bring more people to the company platform for registration and investing, including you.
Me: Okay let me look over your website and social.
JG: Okay, kindly look in it and register, SEND me a screenshot to help you if you have any challenge.
Me: Where are you located?
JG: Tennessee.

{remember their profile said Florida}
Me: What do you do for Disney?
JG: Business Development Strategist.
Me: Yes, I read that on your profile, can you elaborate?
JG: I bring innovation and strategies on it
Me: What takes you to Tennessee?
JG: Disney - I do crypto anytime because I work from my laptop and all trading and investment are been monitored by the company accountant.

{I think now she's suspicious to my questioning}

JG: Why all this?
Me: Just curious.
JG: Nice.
Me: I try to get to know people before I toss out prices. The more I am familiar the better success of any marketing.
JG: Okay nice idea.
JG: What do you have to say yet?
JG: Have you registered on the site yet?
Me: I'll let you know when I do.
JG: Okay.
Me: Are you originally from London? I see the crypto company is set up there?
JG: Send me screenshot so I can understand better what you are saying.
Me: {Sends screenshot of London address from site}
JG: Yes, that's where we have HQ
JG: Did you register on site yet?
Me: No, I'll let you know when I do.

{I guess 3 times saying NO did it}

JG: Okay, I think you will have to leave the marketing job for now, I will let you know when I need it again.

{And I was blocked on WhatsApp, unfriended and blocked on LinkedIn}

The reason I share this dialogue with you is to showcase how a typical scam works. Now you might be thinking, they were just trying to get me to register for their crypto service... and that would be a fair assessment. They use small talk and knowledge gleaned from your profile to get you to share information. Then they try to entice you to sign up for their service. However…their crypto portal requires you to give them your name, address, proof of identity, email, phone number and links to your financial institution. And when they have all your credentials it becomes easier for them to scam you of your money.

And being the dialogue was filled with broken English, phrases not common in the US, and the person not aware their company was based in London are all red flags that people need to be aware of when dealing with unknown connections.

Be curious. Ask questions. If the responses given seem odd or out of place or your Spidey-sense is tingling it's a warning to stay away.

Oh, and she never did buy my books, it was just a ruse to help win me over and get me to register on her crypto website. And being that you can add any job title with any company on your LinkedIn profile, dollars for donuts she didn't work for Disney either. Just a giant scam.

To Be Or Not To Be…Forthright!

My cell rings while I'm outside playing catch with my grandson.

Caller ID displays "Scam"

I answer it anyway…

Me: Hello.

Caller: Hi this is Kaitlyn with Car Warranty Operations

Me: Where?

Kaitlyn: Car Warranty Operations

Me: Okay and?

Kaitlyn: Do you still have a 2013 Chevrolet Suburban?

Me: I never owned a 2013 Suburban.

Kaitlyn: Okay Sir, can you tell me what you are driving now?

Me: Well, I'm not driving anything right now, I'm in my yard throwing a ball with my grandson.

Kaitlyn: No Sir, what vehicle do you own?

Me: I own several, but you wanted to know what I was driving now.

Kaitlyn: {Raises voice} Tell me what vehicle you own!

Me: You sound bossy.

Kaitlyn: I'm losing my patience with you.

Me: Well, ask the right questions next time.

Kaitlyn: Sir, this is important and you are wasting my time.

Me: If this was truly important you would have already known what vehicle I was driving or owning and wouldn't need to ask dumb questions.

Kaitlyn: We will find you.

Me: I already told you I'm in my yard.

Kaitlyn: Sir, I have the feeling you actually own the 2013 Suburban and don't want to be forthright.

Me: Forthright you say? Oh yes, not being forthright to scam callers is exactly what I do.

Kaitlyn: {Curses at me in some foreign language} We will find you.

{She hung up}

Note: Never confirm what vehicle you own to a stranger on the phone. Ever!

Slower And Louder

Ooh...I could lower my electric rate by 30% for the next 18 months says the caller who can barely speak English.

Me: So how does this scam work?

Caller: Sir, what?

Me: Let me repeat it slower... and louder...
HOW - DOES - THIS - SCAM - WORK?

Caller: {curses at me in some foreign language}

Me: You too buddy.

{And he hung up}

Note: This particular day I had received about 35 calls and I was tired. I just didn't have the energy to deal with their shenanigans and thought what the heck let's just cut to the chase and ask the question, "how does this scam work?"

I Need Your Name

Phone rings...caller ID displays "Scam"

Had to answer...it's what I do.

Message plays..."*This is a legal enforcement notice, a warrant has been issued against your name and criminal proceedings have been lodged against you, press 1 to speak to an agent.*"

{So I pressed 1}

{A deep foreign accented male voice answers the phone, although his voice is drowned out by all the other scammers in the call center}

Agent: This is Phil with the Department of Treasury.

Me: Okay...hey... I'm responding to your message.

Agent: Can I get your name?

Me: Can you tell me what this is about?

Agent: I need your name.

Me: And what if I refuse.

Agent: We will arrest you.

Me: Over the phone?

Agent: We know where you live.

Me: Where?

Agent: {gives an address about 50 miles away}

Me: Wow, you're good.

Agent: We are sending officers there now to arrest you.

Me: I'll be waiting.

Agent: Aren't you worried?

Me: Nah, I get these calls every day. And every time I wait. But so far, no one has ever shown up.

Agent: Why are you wasting my time?

Me: You called me. You threatened me with arrest. Yet you never follow through. So who is wasting who's time?

Agent: We will arrest you.

Me: I'm waiting.

{pfft...he hung up}

Note: If you get calls like this...just remember, it's a scam. They won't send people after you, but they will threaten you with arrest. And if you fall for it, most likely they will steal your identity, your money or both.

Henceforth Your Name Is Cheeto

Phone rings...Caller ID displays a local number.

Me: Hello.

Caller: {Says his name really fast and in a foreign accent sounds like Cheeto}

Me: Hi Cheeto.

Caller: My name is {says name again, still sounds like Cheeto) not Cheeto.

Me: Well your name sounds like Cheeto.

Caller: I assure you Sir, it is not Cheeto.

Me: Okay let me ask you, how many people can actually say your name?

Caller: That is inconsequential.

Me: Okay henceforth your name is Cheeto.

Caller: No Sir, I already have a name.

Me: And since nobody can pronounce it, I declared your name to be Cheeto. Accept it.

Caller: F-You A-Hole.

Me: Cheeto I don't think F-You A-Hole is in the script now is it?

Caller: I know where you live.

Me: That's nice.

Caller: I'll be right over to teach you some respect.

Me: I'll be here waiting.

{He hangs up}

{Not even 2 minutes go by and my door bell rings. I'm like "crap, Cheeto meant it". So I open the door}

Me: Are you Cheeto?

Guy at Door: No I'm Tom from Global Solar.

Me: I was expecting Cheeto, have you seen him?

Guy at Door: I don't know a Cheeto.

Me: Okay, what do you want?

Guy at Door: Has anyone ever shown you the benefits of solar?

Me: Yes, yes they have… and several of them are buried in my back yard, would you like to be next?

{I never saw someone run so fast}

{Anyway, I'm still waiting for Cheeto to show up}

Chapter 12

Hey, They're My Superpowers.

"They call me Mr. Sarcasm."

It Depends

Hey Rob, can you fix our website?

Me: It depends.

Them: Depends on what?

Me: How much your website person screwed it up?

Them: Oh.

Me: Can you grant me admin access to the website?

Them: Yeah.

{sends me his username and password}

Me: Great, I will take a look.

{I discover a mess}

Me: Hey, I see that your web person has not updated your plugins or themes in years - you have 38 update notices.

Them: Can you fix?

Me: Yup.

Them: Do it.

Me: Done.

{10 minutes later web guy sends client a message asking if he or someone using his sign-in information accessed the site, then he blocked the owner from accessing his own site}

Them: The web guy didn't like that you updated the site and kicked me out, what do I do?

Me: Fire him and demand access to your site.

{An hour goes by}

Them: Hey I talked to my web guy he unblocked me and apologized.

{I sign back in and all the changes and updates I made are gone}

Me: I see your web person dialed back my updates and changes and put your site back how it was before I fixed it.

Them: What? Why would he do that? Can you fix?

Me: Yup, but he might pull the same crap and rollback after I fix it.

Them: Just fix it.

Me: Done.

{And web guy does the same thing again.}

Me: You need to fire this guy.

Them: Why is he doing this to me?

Me: No idea...but with every time I fix it, your invoice goes up.

Them: That's not fair.

Me: What's not fair is your web person holding you hostage and costing you money.

Them: I will talk to him.

Me: I'll be here holding my breath.

Them: What's that supposed to mean?

Me: Oy, hopefully the 3rd fix is the last fix.

{It's been several weeks since this interaction and no word back.}

Note: Holding a client hostage is a jerk move…sadly, it's becoming an acceptable behavior…one I will not tolerate. And if I see you doing it, I will call you out. And I hope others call you out too.

Indian Voice

So earlier I was taking my daughter to a party and she punches the address into her phone's GPS.

Her iPhone starts giving directions and I'm thinking that voice sounds familiar.

She said it's an Indian accent. She said it's a relaxing voice.

I say it sounds like my buddy Parthiv Shah. I was waiting for the GPS voice to say "thank you very much, that'll be $5."

Well I shared that interaction on Facebook.

And it didn't take long for Parthiv to respond..

"I will be sending you an invoice. Did you know invoice is short for INdian VOICE."

Note: I've mentioned Parthiv in some of my other Rob Versus books…and he's become a trusted advisor, a friend and someone I can refer business to. And he's funny also. To learn more about Parthiv head on over to www.elaunchers.com

No Hortons For Me

Hey Rob, can I help you?
{Message received thru Facebook chat}

Me: I didn't ask for help.

Them: Yes of course, but I think I can help you.

Me: Okay, can you get me a vanilla ice coffee?

Them: I'm not a Horton's coffee server.

Me: Well, that's a shame.

Them: Why is that?

Me: You really want to help me, but are not willing to get me a vanilla iced coffee.

Them: I don't offer that kind of help.

Me: What type of help were you offering then?

Them: I can help you with getting more clients.

Me: And you don't think I can do that without your help?

Them: Do you want to know more or not?

Me: I'll choose the or not option.

Them: Can I email you more information?

Me: That doesn't seem like an or not option.

Them: Okay I found your email and just sent you the info.

Me: Yeah, I just deleted it.

Them: Why?

Me: Didn't ask for it.

Them: But I think I can help you.

Me: Here's how you can help...get me a vanilla iced coffee.

{And I got blocked.}

Note: I do indeed like a good vanilla iced coffee…so if you ever wish to help me…that's probably a good place to start.

Third Time

Grr...random message drops in my messenger chat box.

"Hi Rob, we would like to interview you on our podcast, we have you scheduled for {gives a date on a Sunday at lunch time}."

Me: {thinking WTF is this and how dare they assume I'm available for that time, so I respond} That's a Sunday, no can do.

Them: But our podcast is fantastic and we want you on it.

Me: Not sure you understood my reply, so I'll repeat it. That's a Sunday, no can do.

Them: But our podcast is listened to by over 500 thousand people.

Me: Well, that's nice.

Them: So you will agree to be on it.

Me: Not on a Sunday.

Them: But that's when we record it.

Me: Then you'll record without me.

Them: I don't understand, this is a good opportunity.

Me: Is it though? I mean seriously you assumed I would be available on a day and time you scheduled and that I would say yes. So I will say for a third time...that's a Sunday, no can do.

Them: Okay, you can't do Sunday, is there a day that works better?

Me: You know, you should have lead with that. Would have simplified this whole convo, but nooooo! You had to assume.

{And I got blocked}

I suppose Third Time was a Charm.

Note: Boundaries people. Learn to establish boundaries. You have to learn to separate your personal life from your work life. Sadly though, some just assume since you are an entrepreneur you're available anytime. Nah, that's not how it works.

Apparently You Are Calling Me Obnoxious

"Hey Rob are you going to the event in Florida next week?"
{Message received thru Facebook chat}

Me: Nope.

Them: Why not?

Me: {Me already knowing how this conversation is going to go and mentally preparing myself} Don't want to.

Them: Why would you not?

Me: Well let's see... (1) Don't feel like it, (2) I've heard all the speakers before (3) I didn't buy tickets to it (4) I never made plane or hotel reservations and (5) There will be too many obnoxious people there asking me stupid questions.

Them: I'll be there.

Me: Yup.

Them: So apparently you are calling me obnoxious and stupid.

Me: Only if you feel that way.

Them: WTF man...I ask about the event and you go all rude on me.

Me: Did I though?

Them: Yes you called me obnoxious and stupid.

Me: I said there will be too many obnoxious people there asking me stupid questions. And you assumed I was talking about you.

Them: You were.

Me: You are here being obnoxious and stupid - I can't imagine what you will act like at the event.

Them: Your an a-hole.

Me: It's you're (as in "you are").

Them: I don't care, I'm glad you are not going.

Me: Me too.

Them: I'm unfriending you.

Me: Smartest thing you've done all day.

{Wait for it...}

Them: F You

{And he unfriended and blocked me}

Note: Triggering people is my superpower. And with great power comes great sarcastic responsibility.

About The Author

Rob is affectionately known as "Mr. Sarcasm" to his friends - to everyone else he's a Certified Digital Marketing Strategist, a Foremost Expert On Specialized SEO, a Serial Author, Podcaster, Speaker and Authority Broadcaster who can help amplify YOU to your audience.

Rob has also produced books for many clients including lawyers, doctors, copywriters, speakers and consultants.

Rob helps companies across the globe generate new revenue and capture online business. And he hates scammers with a passion.

Rob is available to share talks and give interviews.

To learn more about Rob visit **www.AnspachMedia.com** or call Anspach Media at **(412)267-7224** today.

Resources

THE INTERVIEW SERIES FOR ENTREPRENEURS

Rob Anspach interviews talented entrepreneurs who demonstrate an eagerness to share their experiences, their knowledge and their stories to help others succeed.

Listen to the Rob Anspach's E-Heroes Podcast today.

Available on:

Apple, Google, I Heart Radio, Stitcher, Spotify, Pandora

Or

www.AnspachMedia.com

Rob Versus The Scammers

Protecting The World Against Fraud, Nuisance Calls & Downright Phony Scams.

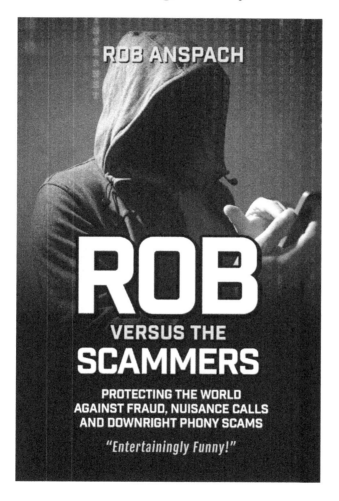

Available on Amazon in Print & Kindle
www.RobVersus.com

Rob Versus The Morons

Overcoming Idiotic Customers With Wit, Sarcasm And A Take No Bullshit Attitude

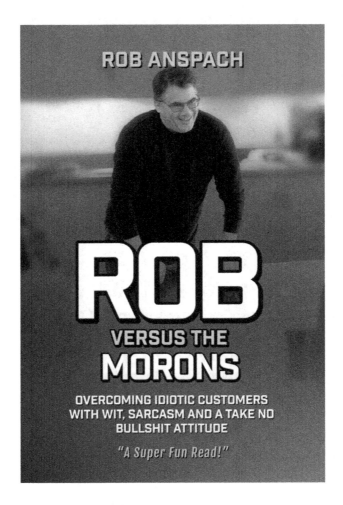

Available on Amazon in Print & Kindle
www.RobVersus.com

Rob Versus Humanity

The Last Line Of Defense In Outwitting, Outlasting and Outliving Time Wasters, Fraudsters And Fools.

Available on Amazon in Print & Kindle
www.RobVersus.com

Rob Versus The Entitled

Defeating The Aggressive, Offended, And Easily Triggered With A Little Common Sense & A Lot Of Sarcasm.

Available on Amazon in Print & Kindle
www.RobVersus.com

Rob Versus The Whackadoos

Conquering Ridiculous Attitudes and Scammy Behaviors With Lightning Fast Wit & Shearing Sarcasm.

Available on Amazon in Print & Kindle
www.RobVersus.com

Other Books By Rob Anspach

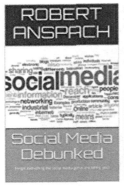

Available on Amazon in Print & Kindle.

www.amazon.com/author/robertanspach

Books Produced By
Anspach Media
That You Might Enjoy

To learn more visit https://AnspachMedia.com/books

Remember to…

Share This Book!

Share it with your friends!

Share it with your colleagues!

Share it with law enforcement!

Share it on social media.

Share it using this hashtag...

#RobVersusTheUnicorns

Made in the USA
Middletown, DE
19 September 2022

10233295R00086